Introduction

The art of making poseable wooden animals and characters has been practiced for generations, with deep roots in folk art and puppetry. The tilt of the head, the position of the arm, or how a leg is folded will suddenly bring a piece to life and give your creation a personality that is not always achievable with a one-piece carving.

Over the years I've created countless poseable characters, from tiny chipmunks and frogs to my largest wood creation to date, a life-size bear. With each new project, I look for designs that challenge me as a woodworker and carver as well as an artist and designer. I spend a lot of time at the workbench experimenting with different angle cuts, facial expressions, and ways to paint and finish a piece to give each creation as much personality as possible.

My overall goal with the *Croaker* is to mimic the movement and stance of a real-life frog sitting by the pond's edge. I've learned over the years that although my designs are simple, the importance of the joint angles and placement of the hardware are critical if you wish to create a piece that truly portrays the character of the subject.

As with any creative project, it's important that you express your own artistic style, use your preferred tools and materials, and work at the pace most comfortable for you. Make sure to follow the rear leg patterns carefully in order to create leg pieces that will easily collapse together and pose as though the frog is getting ready for a big jump.

This guide to making your very own *Croaker* will take you through the entire creative process, from picking out the best wood to imparting an irresistibly warm and whimsical personality through painting and finishing. In total, you will be making 11 pieces, each of which will help you develop your skills as a carver while giving you a new way to express your creativity.

I hope you find the process of making your very own *Croaker* as enjoyable as I have.

Amazing Frog Facts:

- There are over 5,000 frog species in the world. They are found on every continent except Antarctica.
- Each frog has a unique call; some frog calls can be heard a mile away.
- Croaking is used by male frogs as a way to attract females.
- Frogs don't need to drink water as they absorb it through their skin.
- Some frogs can jump over 20 times their own body length; that translates to a human jumping 30m.
- Every year that a frog goes into hibernation, a new layer of bone forms.
- Frogs have teeth on their upper jaw, which they use to keep their prey in one place until they can swallow it.
- The world's largest frog is the goliath frog of West Africa—it can grow to 15" (38.1cm) and weigh up to 7 pounds.
- Toads are frogs. The word "toad" is usually used for frogs that have warty and dry skin, as well as shorter hind legs.

Choosing the Right Wood

Choose a wood variety that is easy to carve but strong enough hold eye screws without the risk of pulling out.

Basswood

Pro: Basswood is one of the most popular woods for many carvers, because it is easy to cut and control without having to apply many high-pressure cuts. This variety is notable for its tight, consistent grain and relatively uniform coloring.

Con: The softness of the wood may not hold your eye screws securely, especially if your finished piece will be handled often.

Poplar ✔Recommended

Pro: Poplar is not as soft as basswood but can be easily carved by hand. It also holds eye screws more securely.

Con: It's not always easy to find large blocks of poplar. For many projects, you may need to laminate several panels together, adding another day to your project time.

Pine

Pro: Pine is inexpensive and will hold your hardware in place.

Con: You may need to laminate pieces together to form your blank. Pine is a harder wood for carving, and the inconsistent grain can sometimes be challenging for a beginning woodcarver.

Getting Started

Slice the board into four 6" (15.2cm) long pieces. Use a table saw. Glue and stack them, one on top of the other, with the grain moving in the same direction. Apply a generous coating of glue between layers. Then clamp the stack, applying even pressure on both sides to eliminate any gaps. Let dry for at least 12 hours and unclamp.

PREPPING AND ROUGHING OUT

1 **Prepare the blank.** Photocopy the Top View body pattern and attach it to the top of the stack using repositionable spray adhesive. Alternately, you can cut the pattern piece along the perimeter line and trace around it with a pencil or marker.

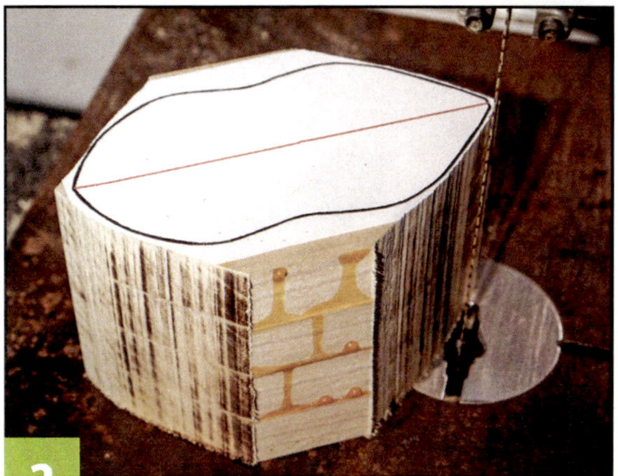

2 **Make the first cuts.** I used a band saw. Remove most of the excess wood in four straight cuts.

3 **Refine the perimeter.** After you've made the corner cuts, make several relief cuts in toward the body side lines. These will allow you to make curved band saw cuts without stressing the blade.

4

Draw the Side View pattern on the side of the blank. Mark the eyes and mouth, as well. Repeat the same cutting process as you used in Steps 2-3. *Note: When cutting around the mouth, first cut straight into the upper lip and then meet that cut from the bottom to form a V-shaped slice in the wood.*

5

Inspect the blank. The back view should look like an even-sided pyramid shape with a clear center and four sides; the front view should have a clear, flat-nosed center area, a small V-shaped valley for the mouth, and four definite sides. The front should also look and feel broader than the back. If necessary, go back to the band saw and refine any areas that can be cut down closer to the lines. Keep the patterns close by, so you can refer to them throughout the carving process.

6

Mark the blank. Draw a centerline from front to back to help keep all markings and cuts symmetrical. Next, with a black marker, mark the corners you'd like to cut away, paying close attention to the final contours shown in the reference images (page 16). Roughly sketch the eye bump areas on the top view, marking the areas you'd like to cut away.

7 **Begin to rough out the body.** You can use a band saw or a rough out knife; I used a band saw. Round the sharp edges, moving from the back of the body to the front. Inspect the blank periodically to make sure the cuts are even. If the shape is uneven, take the time at this stage to even it up with additional shaving cuts.

8 **Rough out the eye area.** Make an angled cut in from one side toward the center of the top of the head. Then come in from the opposite side and meet that cut with a second angled cut to create a V-shaped notch between the eye bumps. Make a couple of shallow shaving cuts to the outside corner of each eye bump. Redraw the eye dot and smile line on both sides of the blank.

CARVING AND SHAPING THE BODY

9 **Shape the mouth.** With a rough out knife, make a stop cut along the entire mouth line, at least 1⁄16" (2mm) deep. Carve up to that line from below, removing wood with small, controlled cuts. Do not remove any wood above the stop cut. Round the bottom edges up from the neck to the mouth line. Remember to inspect the frog often to ensure you are rounding the sides evenly.

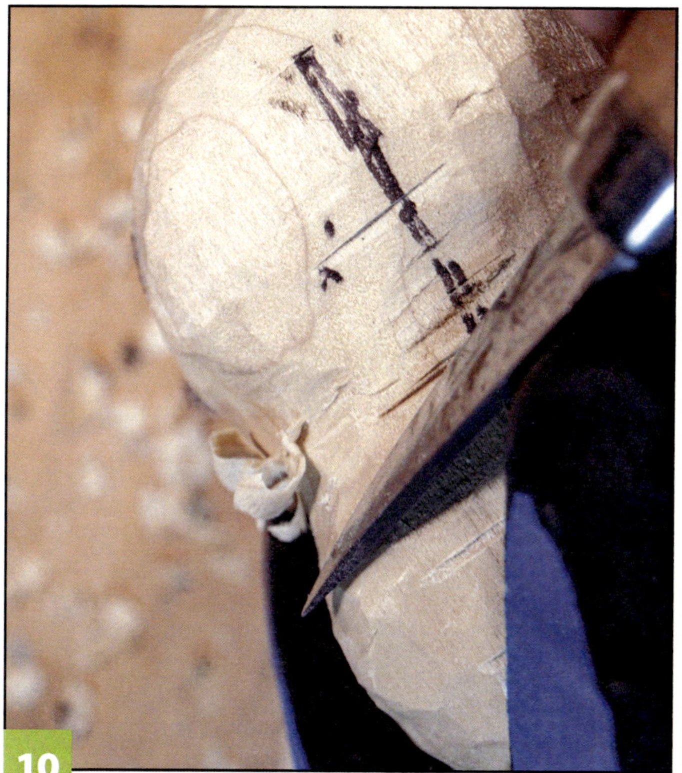

10 **Round the back.** For this part, I slowly turn the frog body in my non-carving hand and begin chipping away the raised areas with short, shallow cuts. Move slowly and steadily, regularly checking for symmetry. With the black marker, mark the areas that will require the most aggressive carving. As you round the piece, remove all remaining marks from the band saw blade.

11 **Refine the back and round the belly.** Make careful paring cuts, pulling the blade toward the thumb of your carving hand. Continue removing sharp corners on all sides until the rump tapers almost to a point in back.

12 **Begin rounding the back and outside areas of the eye bumps.** Remove the wood in small, shallow chips to avoid slicing off too much too quickly.

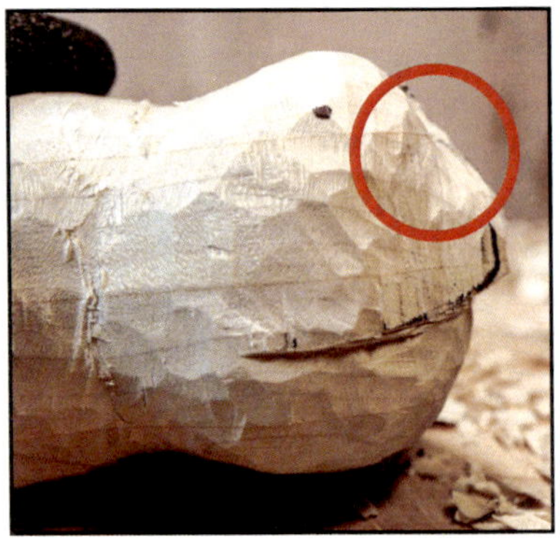

13 **Redraw the eyes and mark the areas to be removed.** Ideally, there should be a dip between the eyes and the top of the mouth; this will give the frog a more expressive look.

14 **Refine the shaping cuts you just made.** At this stage, I like to switch to a smaller, more flexible tool, such as a detail knife. Clean up your cuts all over the body, checking for symmetry and removing any remaining high areas that don't conform to the final shape you want.

MAKING THE ARMS AND LEGS

15 **Attach the arm and leg patterns to a poplar board.** Use repositionable spray adhesive, making sure the grain runs vertically. Cut the pieces on a scroll saw with a #5 reverse-tooth blade or whichever blade size you prefer. *Note: You will cut all leg pieces twice and the front and rear foot pieces once.*

16 **Cut the front and rear feet in half.** Use the band saw or scroll saw.

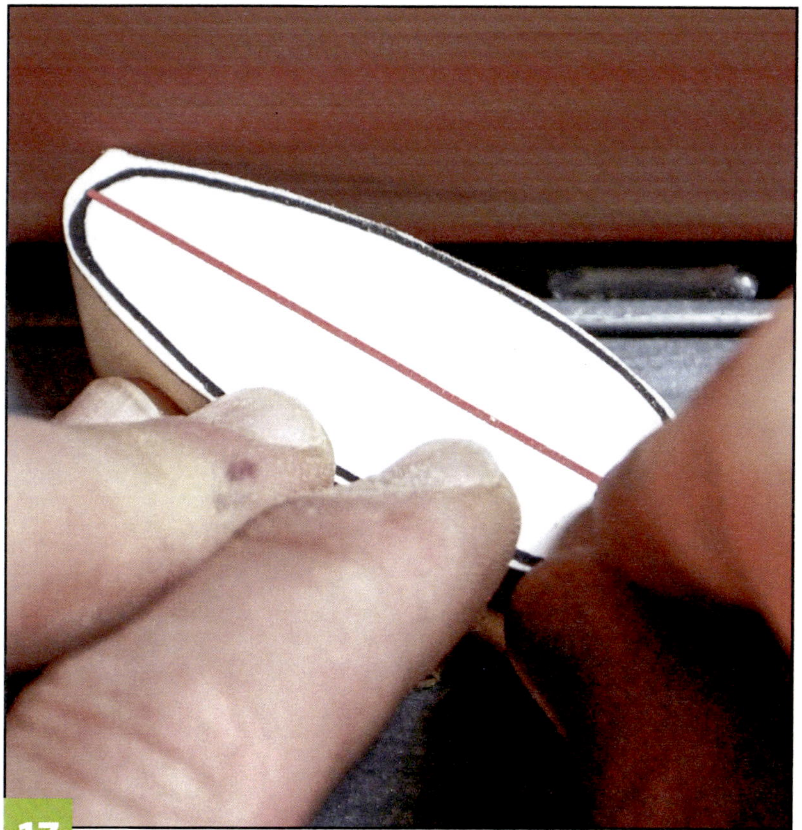

17 **Roughly sand the edges of the feet, hands, and legs.** Use a belt sander. Round the tops and sides of the toes with the belt sander or by hand-sanding, moving up through the grits from 120 to 220.

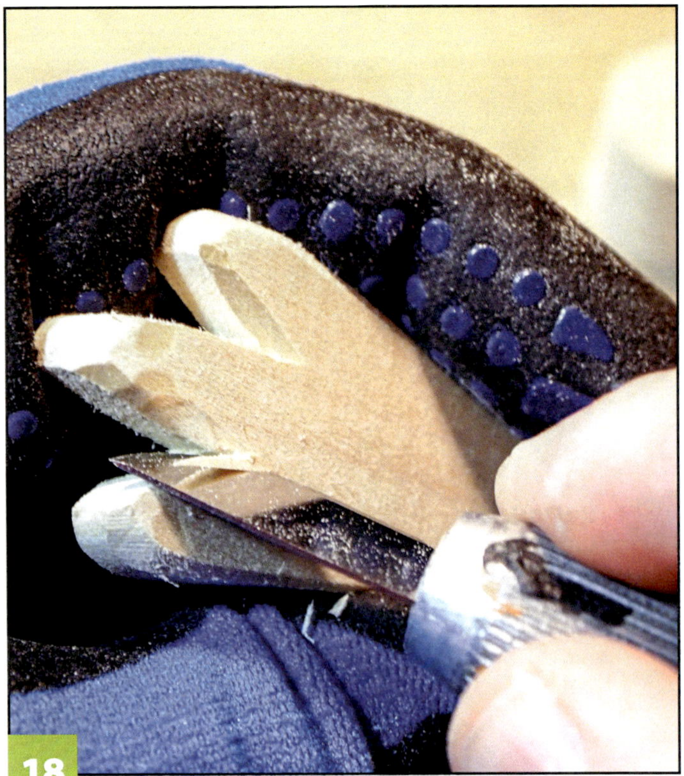

18 **Add definition to the fingers and toes.** I used the detail knife to make a V-shaped cut in each groove.

19 **Draw the side pattern views onto the legs.** The back leg pieces are designed to rest one on top of the other and against the frog's body. Cut them out on the scroll saw, taking special care to follow the lines as closely as possible.

20 **Give the legs a final shape.** Use the band saw to remove any excess wood. Periodically stack the top and bottom pieces together until you remove all space between them, these two elements should fit together like two pieces of a puzzle.

21 **Dry-assemble the frog.** Stack the leg and arm sections and place them against the frog's body to see if any final modifications are necessary.

22 **Carve the finishing touches.** As with the body, proceed to more refined shaping of all leg and arm pieces. Use the detail knife. As you work, remember not to alter the shapes of the elements that need to fit together.

SANDING & ADDING HARDWARE

23 **Sand the torso.** For initial sanding, I suggest a small handheld sander with 100-grit sandpaper, which will quickly begin to smooth the surfaces.

24 **Hand-sand the torso.** I used 150-grit sandpaper. At this stage, pay close attention the mouth line and make any refinements necessary to keep this area smooth and even on both sides. Give the body parts a final sand, moving up gradually through the grits for every piece (limbs and torso) until you reach 800.

25 **Add the hardware.** Use a sharp, pointed awl or nail to create a small starter hole for all eye screws on the body, legs, and feet. A drilled hole is not necessary, since the soft poplar wood will allow you to turn in the handscrews with ease. Turn in the eye screws. Refer to the patterns.

26 **Set up your painting and drying station.** I clamped a wooden dowel rod to the shelves on my worktable for hanging the pieces. I also set aside several small pieces of wire to thread through the eye hooks once the pieces are painted; this way, I can hang the wire at intervals along the dowel rod.

Before You Paint

I prefer to use acrylics for a couple of reasons: they're fast-drying, easy to blend, and will easily accept stains and wax coatings. Remember, these colors will appear lighter when wet. To hold each part for painting, I used small metal hand clamps for the small pieces and vice grips for the torso. When ready to paint, simply grip the eye screw with the clamp or vice grips and hang to dry when complete.

27 **Paint the bottom half.** I used a thinned mixture of sap green and titanium white; I generally thin my paints with water to a 50% dilution. Start with the underside of the mouth line.

28 **Paint the top half.** I used a darker mixture of sap green and titanium white. Apply a generous coat, leaving a small unpainted area between the top and bottom.

29 **Blend the colors.** With a clean brush, begin pulling and blending the two shades of green together with light-handed, horizontal strokes. Keep the brush clean by periodically wiping off excess paint with a paper towel. Once you are satisfied with the level of blending, hang the piece and let dry for at least four hours.

30 **Paint the limbs.** Coat the legs, arms, and feet with the darker shade of green from the top half of the body. Hang and allow these pieces to dry for at least four hours.

31 **Add the details.** Mark the eye placement with a pencil, making sure they are located in the same place on each side. Paint the eyes with a thinned mixture of sap green and burnt umber. Then, using a small detail brush, paint a thin almond-shaped line around each eye.

32 **Add the body spots.** With the same color, begin painting random spots and shapes that follow the curve of the eye bump. Start at the front of the body and work backward, keeping your design relatively symmetrical. As you approach the bottom side and front above the mouth, transition to smaller spots and dots. Hang and allow to dry for four hours.

33 **Add the spots to the limbs.** Using the same technique, add random spots across the surface of the hands and feet. For the arm and leg parts, paint alternating stripes across the tops, sides, and bottom of each piece. Hang and let dry for four hours.

34 **Add depth of color.** At this point, the acrylic finish looks a little too artificial. I prefer to antique my carvings to make them look more natural. Apply a wash of burnt umber and cadmium yellow to the surface of the piece using a large, soft bristle brush. Remove the excess with a clean paper towel. Let each piece dry for at least six hours.

35 **Apply a finish.** To give the frog a shine, rub on a generous amount of traditional floor wax to all the angles of each piece with a rag. Hang and let dry for one hour. Then, hand-rub each piece with cheesecloth.

36 **Assemble the frog.** Open the eye hooks at the end of each leg and arm piece with a pair of needle-nose pliers. Attach the feet to the bottom leg pieces and the bottom leg pieces to the tops. Close the eye screws as you go, using the same tool. Attach the last open eye screws—the ones at the tops of the upper legs—to the rear center eye screw located on the rump. Attach the arms using the same technique. Display as desired.

About the Author

I grew up in the Appalachian Mountains of western Maryland, spending time with my three brothers exploring the mountainsides and creek beds just outside our back door. Our home was a little wood-framed house built by our grandfather in the late '40s, with four rooms, an outhouse by the edge of the woods, and a wood stove in the living room to knock the chill off during the cold winter months. My brothers and I raised chickens, fished, hunted, and trapped, not for entertainment but to help the family through tough times.

When not feeding the chickens, splitting wood, or working in the garden, I spent most of my time drawing, painting, or carving with whatever materials I could find. I loved the creative challenge then as much as I do today.

I was the first in my family to attend college, graduating with a degree in art and design. I feel fortunate to have spent most of my career in creative positions, including several years designing and developing products that made it to the shelves of today's leading gift and garden retailers.

I currently reside near Boiling Springs, Pa., a short walk from the Appalachian Trail. I continue to spend as much of my spare time as possible creating, experimenting, and challenging myself with every new project.

Crazy Croaker Body Patterns

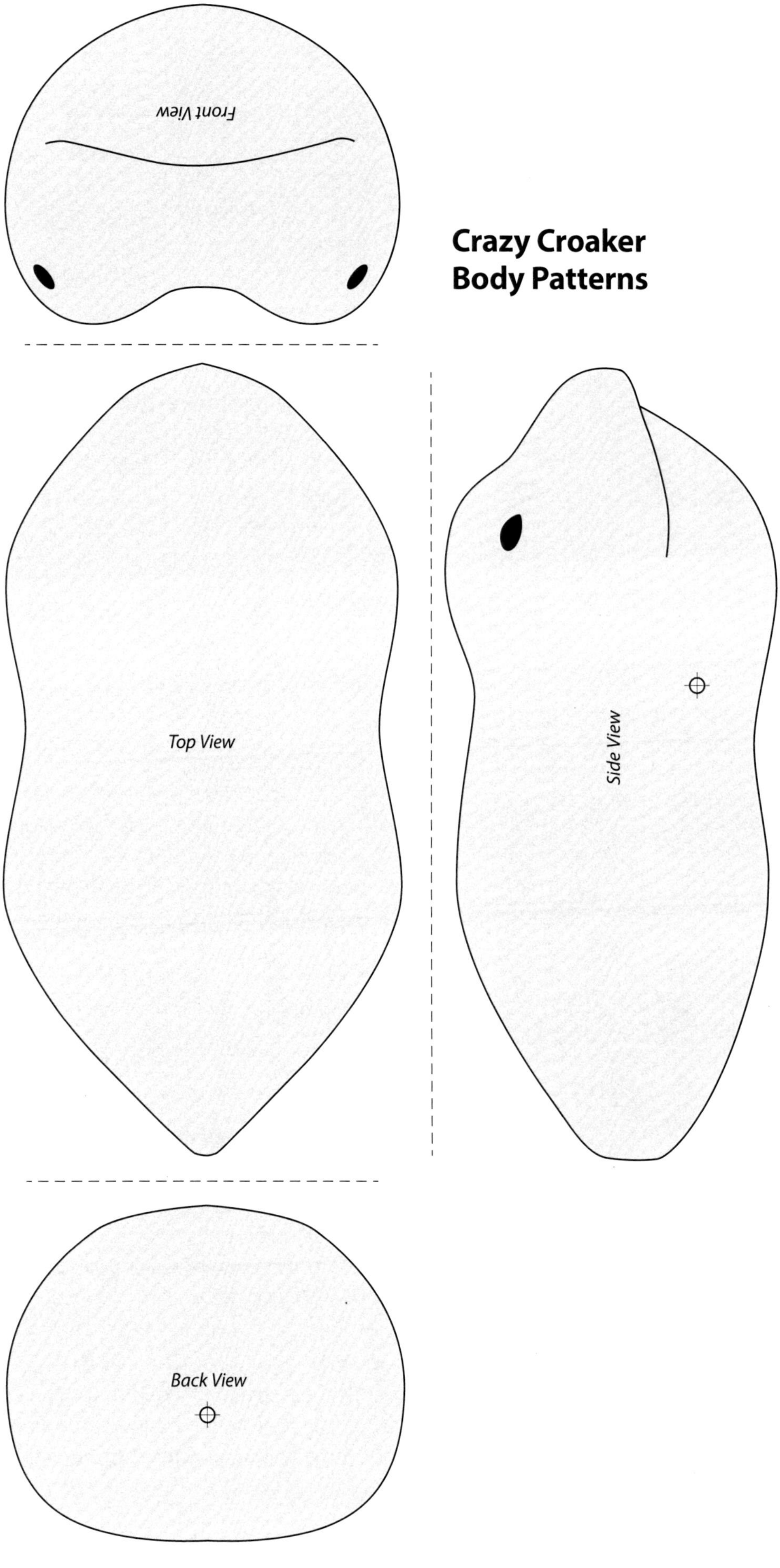

materials & **tools**

MATERIALS

- Poplar, ¾" (1.9cm) thick: 3½" x 32" (8.9cm x 81.3cm)
- Spray adhesive: repositionable
- Pencil or marker
- Wood glue: indoor/outdoor
- Sandpaper: assorted grits
- #214 eye screws, 13⁄16" (2.1cm): 18 each
- #212 eye screw, 15⁄16" (2.4cm): 1 each
- Acrylic paints, such as Grumbacher: burnt umber, cadmium yellow, sap green, titanium white
- Finish, such as Minwax furniture paste
- Paper towels
- Rag
- Cheesecloth
- Wire (optional)

TOOLS

- Band saw (optional)
- Table saw
- Jigsaw or scroll saw with blades: #5 reverse-tooth
- Knives: rough out, detail
- Belt sander (optional)
- Small handheld sander
- Clamps
- Vise grips: 2 each
- Needle-nose pliers
- Paintbrushes: #12 chisel-tip wide soft bristle, #8 round-tip soft bristle

The author used these products for the project. Substitute your choice of brands, tools, and materials as desired.

Crazy Croaker Leg Patterns

Rear Leg Patterns

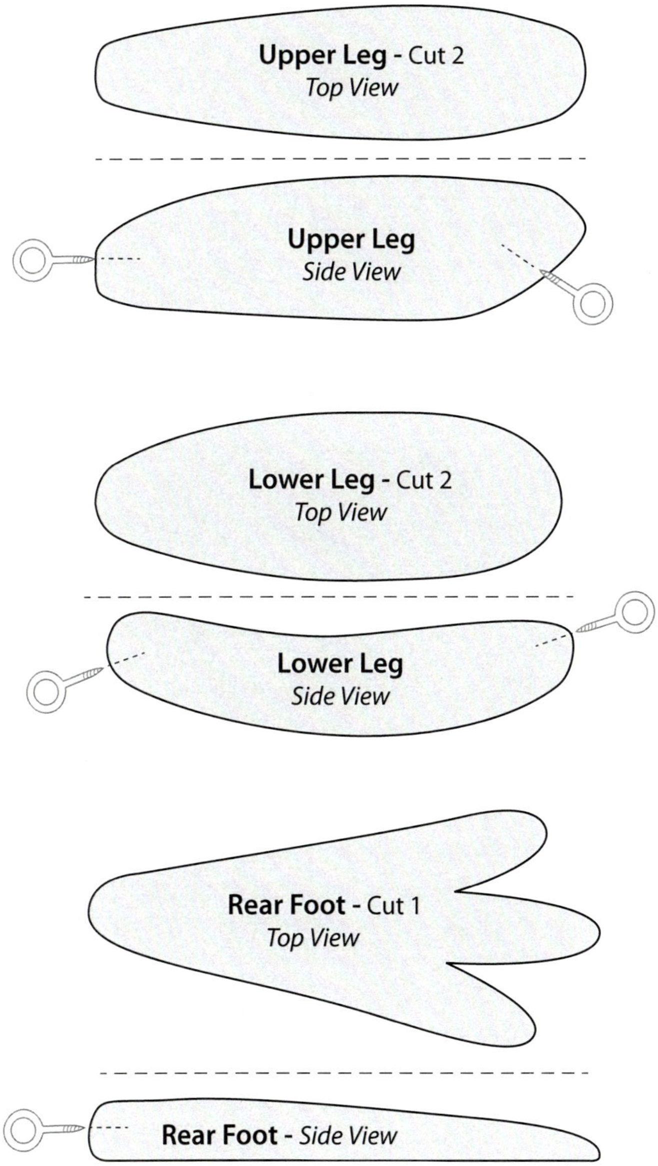

Front Leg Patterns

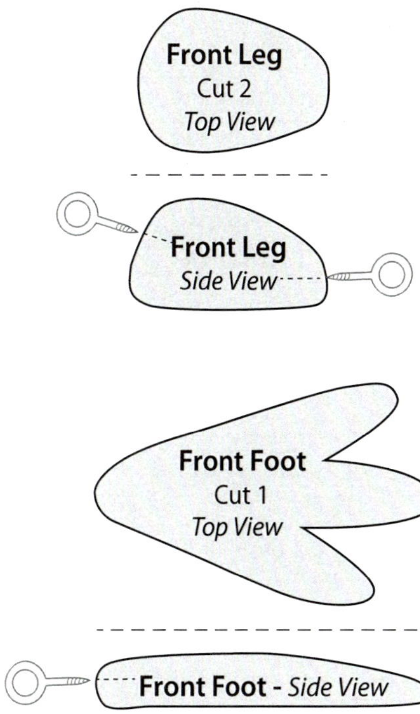